Braving North Korea:

True Stories of Those Secretly Bringing Hope One of the Darkest Nations on Earth

by Scott Croft

Contents:

Preface – Light in the Darkness

This book is about hope. In our overly sensationalized culture, it's become all too easy to focus on crises, never revealing the beautiful light which continually pierces the darkness. Fear sells, but I'm tired of that sinking feeling that comes when a story is left unfinished, when evil seems to have triumphed and hope all but disappears.

I would like to tell a different story.

It's important to understand the background of North Korea, the brokenness of their systems, and the treatment of their people. This book includes a short introduction, which will serve as a framework for our stories. By showing the vastness of the darkness, we have a better reason for cheering when light does emerge. What you will find different about this book is a focus primarily on the beauty inside the brokenness of North Korea through stories dedicated to revealing light where it exists.

The experiences documented in the following pages are true. I have taken the liberty of creatively describing a few details, but have done my best never to compromise the factual integrity of the events. Like most books containing sensitive material, names and locations have been changed to protect those still covertly serving in this hostile area.

May the people you meet throughout the following pages offer as much encouragement to you as they have to me. It's because of their bravery that I remain steadfast in my mission to serve them and to proudly tell their stories.

Scott

Part 1: An Introduction

Chapter 1 – I'm a Smuggler, Nice to Meet You

"How on earth did I wind up here?" The question was rolling around in my head after finishing an exciting Skype call with a good friend and co-worker named Thomas who lives near the border of North Korea and China. It has only been after years of relationship building that Thomas has invited me beyond the surface level into the deep inner workings of his underground operation.

Thomas is a secret agent of sorts and almost everything he does is illegal. Over the last seven years, my friend has managed a successful cross-border smuggling operation into North Korea. He also dabbles in human trafficking.

Now before you close this book and write me off as criminal, let me offer a bit of clarity. Everything Thomas is involved with, he does to offer hope to the people of North Korea. When I tell you he manages a smuggling network, what I mean is that he covertly transports emergency food aid to those facing starvation. As a human trafficker, Thomas does not sell North Koreans into slavery. Instead, he offers those escaping the dark country rescue and relocation services, giving them freedom for the first time as citizens of South Korea. In my eyes, and in the eyes of those he serves, he is a hero.

So how on earth did I, an average guy from rural America, wind up coordinating smuggling and rescue efforts alongside Thomas?

For the last decade, I've worked with grassroots organizations to serve persecuted Christians. It has been my role to help resource an entire network of brave men and women like Thomas who every day risk their lives to ensure hope for those suffering for their faith. I work with friends in Myanmar who rescue believers from genocide. I've coordinate efforts with friends in China working to secretly train and equip new pastors in the explosive growth of the house church movement. I also oversee relationships across the Middle East involved in ministry so covert that their work can't be mentioned in this book.

In this incredible day and age, I can be involved in these missions anywhere in the world with Internet access. Multiple times a year, I have the incredible privilege of traveling to the above-mentioned locations to secretly meet face-to-face with the operatives.

Exciting, right? I fully agree, and yet I almost chose a different path.

As a senior in high school, I distinctly felt God asking me to be a missionary. I had missionaries for grandparents and assumed this calling on my life was the mandate to take up their legacy. But growing up in a materialistic region of America can leave a young man comfortable with his environment. My initial response to God was, "No way! You got the wrong guy." In my mind, full time missions meant leaving everything behind to live in poverty on the plains of some distant country.

Running from God hurts. There comes a point in your fight with heaven when you either submit or go mad trying to ignore that always-present voice. I resisted the call for almost a year. Finally, with tears running down my cheeks, I looked over a large world map spread across my bedroom wall and waved my white flag of surrender. In defeat I waited for the inevitable directive to sell all my possessions and board a plane for the middle of nowhere.

The directive never came. Instead, the Lord took my surrendered heart and led me through a nine-year preparation season, developing in me a genuine love for others around the world. I spent time in jobs that took me to the Far East as well as small desert towns. In each location I was given the gift of incredible community, men and women who loved God and taught me what a relationship with Him truly looked like. I learned how hard loving people can be and how hard it is to serve with unconditional love. But I also gained the will power to stay steady in the effort.

An unwilling missionary can still be used by God, but one who is authentic in the desire to love and serve the people they are called to brings God delight. I needed to become the latter.

Something else happened in those shaping years. I began to lose my white-knuckled grip on comfort. New passions replaced my fear-driven desire to remain in environments I could control. In my younger years I had created boundaries around the city neighborhoods I knew in an attempt to keep my world familiar and easy. As more time passed, my boundaries began to expand and then slowly fade altogether. Traveling to new places around the world became exciting opportunities for adventure. The Lord knew I would need this development for the work He had prepared for me.

After my Skype call with Thomas, my decade long journey began to take new shape. I suddenly became aware of an enormous gratitude I felt. My life purpose was now to serve people groups around the world, even in seemingly unreachable places. I guess that makes me a missionary.

I believe all of us will face a crisis of comfort if we truly want to follow Christ. One day you may be called out of your small fishing boat onto turbulent seas. In those moments you will have to make the choice to leave comfortable behind. But Jesus waits, out among the waves, offering us "life to the full."

Who knows, He might even call you to North Korea.

I wish I could tell you that mission work in North Korea is easy. Honestly, it's the exact opposite. Serving North Korea can leave one feeling as though they are standing on the edge of a giant precipice. You begin to wonder if your small bucket of light can really make a difference in the immense darkness before you.

The good news is that, in spite of the circumstances, over the last decade I've watched God take our little bit of light and amplify it a thousand times over to bring hope to more people than I could ever have thought possible.

Understanding the basics of the country's disorder might better help you appreciate the way God is amplifying light. If you are unfamiliar with North Korea, this will be a great base layer to begin your journey.

A common question arises when I tell others about my line of work:

"Why are the rescue and aid services you support so opposed? If there are needy people inside North Korea, why doesn't the government allow outsiders to bring in food and other resources?"

The answer to this question sheds light on the entire breakdown of the North Korean system ... pride.

So where does this pride come from? Let's take a step backward and look at the history of North Korea.

The Korean people have faced severe oppression for centuries. The small Asian peninsula has defended itself time and time again from invaders in an effort to maintain its independence. Sadly, many of those wars were lost.

After World War II and the Korean conflict, the peninsula was separated into two countries. The Soviet Union backed the North while the American and Allied forces backed the South. This was a critical juncture for the Korean people, setting the course for the next 60 years of divided life between the two nations.

The Soviet Union placed Kim Il Sung in power over the North and helped establish a communist system under his leadership. Instead of offering a new era of liberation to his people, Kim Il Sung all but eradicated the Christian faith of his parents and set up a system to worship himself as the great savior. Since the beginning of his reign, the North Korean people have been forced into an unrelenting devotion to the Kim dynasty. Failure to literally bow to idols of past and present leaders can result in a death sentence.

Though the Christian faith was never fully obliterated, believers have been forced to go underground. Many experts still believe North Korea is the worst country in the world for persecuting followers of Jesus. Simply possessing a Bible can result in a labor camp sentence for both the owner as well as their immediate family up to three generations.

Religious oppression was only the beginning of Kim Il Sung's failures. Part of his self-deification included promoting himself as the ultimate provider. Kim developed the ideology of Juche, meaning self-reliance, and began to pull away from allies as well as cutting off foreign trade. The downward economic spiral had begun.

By cutting itself off from outside aid, North Korea quickly began consuming what little natural resources it had to sustain its population. Worse, Kim began investing heavily in weapons and armament, including nuclear technology, diverting desperately needed funding away from agricultural development. Although state run media outlets still praised Kim Il Sung, his decisions had sealed a death sentence for millions of people.

Between 1994 and 1998 the economic crisis reached a climax.

Flooding and droughts served as the "final straw," almost completely collapsing the entire North Korean system. Actual numbers are hard to obtain with the country closed off from the outside world, but many experts estimate that up to 3.5 million people died in the 90's from starvation and illness caused by malnutrition. That's over 15 percent of the country's estimated population of 23 million.

The worst of the famine has since passed, but things are still far from optimal in North Korea. Those able to pass along information from inside the sealed borders report severe food shortages, sparse electricity, and insufficient heat. The current government relies heavily on allied foreign aid but uses most of those resources to support the army, ignoring the people needing it the most. Recent reports indicate North Korea could have provided supplemental food for the entire country for a year with funds spent on just one rocket test for its nuclear program.

"If things are so bad for the common citizen, why isn't there an uprising?"

Cut off from the outside world, North Korea's people rely on state run media outlets for their news. The reports by officials are fabricated to spread the regime's propaganda. Citizens are continually fed the lie that their country exists in the best possible state, that the Kim dynasty has unparalleled wisdom to lead and provide, and that life outside the borders is much, much worse. Though people are suffering every day from malnutrition, most believe the world outside would offer a much quicker death sentence.

North Korea's borders are not completely impenetrable. Rumors of the truth are slowly spreading. For this reason, the punishment for defection has been elevated. In recent years, guards have been ordered to shoot and kill anyone trying to escape through North Korea's northern border into China.

Fleeing Koreans, fortunate enough to make it into China without being shot, face new dangers of being found by secret police. Hundreds of North Korean undercover officers have been dispatched into border cities with the sole purpose of hunting citizens who have escaped. When found, defectors are brought back inside North Korea in chains where they face a labor camp sentence or even a firing squad.

Pride can cause so much unneeded brokenness and suffering. In the case of North Korea, it has led to an entire country on the brink of collapse.

You can understand why at the beginning of the chapter I gave the analogy of standing next to a dark precipice. Yet even in the face of such grave circumstances, there are those who are risking all to bring life and hope to the country of North Korea. Now that you understand the challenges they face, let's begin our journey through the stories of those I am privileged to work alongside every day.

Part 2: Breaking In

Chapter 3 — The Toughest Woman I Know

Standing at just over five feet tall, Debra doesn't appear to be someone who would fearlessly undermine one of the most hostile government regimes on the planet. Every time I'm with this incredible woman, I have to remind myself what her soft demeanor hides. She is one of the most successful North Korean smugglers I work alongside.

Debra continues to run secret operations at an age in life when danger should be well behind her. Using time-tested covert methods, she frequently crosses China's border into North Korea. She is able to bring life-sustaining food, medicine and clothing to a network of North Korean Christian families in desperate need.

Debra's brave story spans over 20 years of faithful service. During the great famine of the 90s, Debra began to hear God's voice leading her to help the desperate people living just miles from her home in China. God's words remained an ever-present stirring in her heart: *"I want you to go to North Korea."*

When she finally had enough courage to tell her family of the new mandate on her life, they immediately tried to convince her otherwise. Over and over she would hear the words, *"There is too much danger involved."* Despite the resistance from those closest to her, Debra knew she would not be deterred.

Not knowing where to start, Debra decided to carry a 40-pound bag of rice across a frozen section of the river that separates China and North Korea. Arriving for the first time illegally inside the country she had been called to reach, the mother now turned smuggler headed straight to the nearest village.

A small home located on the edge of town looked like a good place to start. The couple that answered the door was shocked as they stared at the foreigner on their doorstep holding more rice than they had seen in years. Although Debra's Korean language differed slightly from the couple's dialect, she was able to explain that she had brought the food as a gift from the other side of the river. Then, as stealthily as she had come, Debra slipped back across the border.

Over the next few months, Debra made return visits to the same home, each time bringing them rice as well as other small living supplies. Finally one evening the couple, who she now knew as Joon and Hana, begged her to come in and stay for awhile. Debra agreed but remained vigilant, knowing that the pair was risking their lives to host her.

In hushed tones the three talked. The couple pressed Debra with questions about her gifts. Never before had they or those they knew been shown such generosity. They could not comprehend why someone they had never met would go to great lengths to offer them kindness.

In the late evening hour, Debra shared her faith in Jesus with the couple and told them of her call to offer hope to the people of North Korea. With tears in her eyes Hana revealed that she was a believer in Jesus but had been forced to keep her faith a secret, even from her beloved husband.

Debra knew what Hana had just done by revealing this forbidden information. By North Korean law, Joon was now obligated to turn his wife in to the authorities. She would be sentenced to a labor camp for the crime of being a follower of Jesus Christ. But Joon only smiled as he looked lovingly at his wife. *"If faith in Jesus led this woman to our door, then He must be the true savior,"* he said reassuringly.

Experiencing a new courage in their faith, Hana and Joon began mirroring Debra's generosity with their extended family and neighbors using portions of the aid they had been given. Although the evangelism effort would surely bring a death sentence if discovered by officials, the message of the Gospel began to spread.

By the time Debra was able to return, many in the village had already become Christians. Hana and Joon shared the incredible news and asked if she would meet to disciple some of the new believers. Debra was not a teacher, and although feelings of inadequacy plagued her, she agreed to spend time with those desperate to grow in their new faith.

This time, as Debra crossed back over the border, she knew her small operation was in need of growth. No longer would a single bag of rice be enough. An entire village was experiencing poverty and hunger. She knew she would have to find a way to increase her efforts.

Twenty years later, Debra now aids over 200 families. Most are secret Christians who have given their lives to Jesus as a result of the food and discipleship. The evangelism efforts started through Hana and Joon are now growing exponentially.

Carrying bags of rice across the river has long since ceased to be an effective method for Debra to enter North Korea. Over the years, she has cleverly developed alternative systems. Her covert techniques now allow her to carry multiple tons of food, clothes, and medicine to her underground network. Trusted leaders have been identified among the villages she serves, all of whom work alongside her to ensure the aid reaches those most in need.

But her efforts have not been without consequence. On multiple occasions, Debra has been arrested and even beaten inside North Korea. By God's grace, she has always been released and after shifting her methods and identity, she returns more impassioned as a result.

On the rare occasions when I am able to be in the same room with Debra, I am always humbled. With tears in her eyes, this incredible lady shares her reports with messages of deep gratitude from the underground church she serves. From her unique vantage point, she sees just how important it is that the church around the world supports her mission to bring aid and the gospel to North Korea.

I risk very little to do my part in telling her story and raising support for her shipments. In my mind, all the gratitude should be offered to her and the Lord for what He is able to do with such a willing servant. She is the true hero and the bravest woman I know.

Chapter 4 – In the Nick of Time

"LORD, you are the God who saves me;
day and night I cry out to you.
May my prayer come before you;
turn your ear to my cry."
Psalm 88:1-2 (NIV)

The stories Debra shared have grown in number as her aid operations took her beyond Hana and Joon's village. Each story contained a common thread ... hope birthed in the midst of deep darkness. Euni's story in particular stands out as an example of God's loving care over the people of North Korea.

Like most of her community, Euni's family had found themselves in desperation. Fears of starvation consumed their every waking moment. On a day when hope had almost completely been lost, Debra had shown up at their home. Euni's village was in a remote area that Debra had bravely ventured to reach. It was the last stop along an exploratory route to develop new areas of North Korea.

Debra had reached the end of her journey but feared the small portion of remaining aid would barely suffice for one family. Euni thought differently. To her family, the foreigner standing at their door looked like an angel holding enough food to prepare a feast.

It took just one visit from Debra to convince Euni that Jesus was the path to salvation. Her country's leader had failed to provide, but through Debra God had shown Himself to be a true Father. Overcome with emotion, Euni became a Christian that very day.

Euni's family continued to worship Jesus in secret, praying for His continued provision. Because of their location, Debra could only bring occasional aid deliveries. Every grain of rice was received with joyful gratitude.

As time passed, North Korean security grew tighter, making many of the remote areas along Debra's route too risky for visits from outsiders. It had been three years since she had been able to visit Euni's village and the family's food resources had been almost completely wiped out. One morning, Euni awakened to find that she could barely get out of bed. Her health had rapidly declined due to malnutrition.

Using an underground system established by the growing network of Christians along Debra's route, Euni sent a message asking for the smuggler to once again find a way back to her family. Euni's prayers grew desperate as she pleaded for the message to arrive safely.

Her note described a secret time and place outside her village where Debra had met with the family on numerous occasions. Euni believed that the seclusion would offer greater protection for a visit but she also knew that Debra would still be taking great risks by coming so far into North Korea once again.

By God's grace, Euni's note indeed made it to its recipient. Upon receiving news of the family's dire situation, Debra immediately prepared for the dangerous journey. She gathered food, cooking oil, and even cold weather clothing to ensure the family would survive the approaching winter. As soon as she was able, Debra slipped quietly across the North Korean border and began making her way toward the location Euni had described.

On the date set in her message, Euni arrived at the meeting place clinging to every shred of hope that her prayers had been answered. Entering a small clearing, Euni once again came face to face with the woman who had saved her life. Debra, standing with the aid she had brought, reached out to embrace her longtime friend. Euni could no longer hold in her emotions and burst into tears as she threw her arms around Debra. It was a beautiful reunion, full of gratitude that the Lord had provided rescue once again.

Chapter 5 – Paying It Forward

After a decade of missions inside North Korea, Debra had grown her aid network beyond what she had ever thought possible. Her visits had become more frequent, and as a result trusted families had opened their homes to provide safe lodging while she visited those along her route.

It was during a stay in one of these homes that Debra's distribution efforts nearly came to a screeching halt. Philip, a relative of the family Debra was staying with, had decided to come by for a visit. He entered the home expecting to greet his sister. Instead, he found a stranger who was obviously uncomfortable at being discovered.

Philip's first thought on finding a Chinese woman secretly hiding in the house was to call the authorities and have her arrested. He knew the entire family was in jeopardy for having contact with a foreigner and could be thrown in a prison camp. He was angry and scared as he confronted his sister, but something in her eyes changed his accusations.

Philip listened as his sister described Debra's mission. Then, as he saw the amount of food that the smuggler had brought to give away, the last of his reservations faded. He struggled to understand why this woman would risk her life to bring help to his starving family and community. It was a perfect opportunity for Debra to share the gospel with him. Philip was overcome with emotion and accepted Christ as his savior.

Debra had enough food to give a portion to Philip to take back to his family. It had been months since his wife and parents had been able to eat a full meal. Philip not only had food, but also a new faith to share. Soon the entire family became believers.

Each time Debra covertly entered North Korea, she made sure to bring an additional aid portion for Philip's family. Slowly their lives began to change. Before long, Philip knew he could no longer keep his secret to himself. Just like his sister, he had to risk his life and share his newfound faith and food with others he loved who were in desperate need.

Debra agreed to provide an additional amount with each trip that could be used in the new evangelism efforts. Using the extra food he received, Philip carefully looked for opportunities to begin reaching out to his neighbors. He prayed that those he chose would see the offering as a gift and accept both the physical and spiritual nourishment he had to offer. He also prayed that his secret acts would not be exposed to local authorities.

Modern Day:

Philip now has two children, a daughter and a son. With Debra's help, Philip has brought thirty new families into the aid network, ensuring their survival through the famines North Korea constantly endures. His evangelism efforts continue and I'm looking forward to the many more brothers and sisters in Christ who believe as a result of his secret outreach.

Charity looked over her shoulder again at the cart she had strapped to her bicycle. She had double-checked all the connections but each bump in the road gave her concern. It was imperative her precious cargo remain safe. She could not afford to lose even a single item.

The small sacks of rice, oil, soap, and medicine were secure and she breathed a sign of relief. Back in her village, 30 North Korean Christian families were waiting patiently for her return. Without the contents of her cart, most of those families would face starvation.

Charity is one of Debra's secret partners living inside North Korea. Debra's network had quickly expanded over the years to include many families in multiple locations. Debra could no longer handle the workload on her own and knew it was time to trust others with the mission. Charity, who had shown incredible promise in her Christian growth and desire to aid her extended family and neighbors, became one of the first to be discipled by Debra.

Debra continued to bring large shipments of emergency resources into the closed country, but began using a safe staging area centrally located within traveling distance from the villages she served. Charity, along with other leaders Debra had identified, made the journey by bicycle or on foot. The staging area provided shelter for Debra to spend multiple days offering intense discipleship for each leader that arrived. Then, carts were loaded with enough aid to provide support for a leader's entire village until Debra could again return.

Every time Charity takes the long bike ride, she is reminded of what she risks. It has only been a few years since her family was turned over to authorities by scared neighbors who discovered they were Christians.

The fate of Charity's family is a common threat for believers inside North Korea. The government threatens prison for citizens who have knowledge of Christian activity but fail to report the illegal practice. Sometimes this even happens within families when a Bible or other contraband is discovered. Better one family member in prison then three generations punished.

For one year, Charity's relatives were locked away. They suffered beatings and their bodies decayed from malnutrition and lack of medical care. Charity's brother-in-law eventually succumbed to the torture and died from the abuse he had sustained. When Charity received word of his passing, she was devastated. Her only thoughts were of how to rescue her sister and nephew from the same fate.

I learned of Charity's sister when it appeared all was lost. Charity had reached out to Debra in a desperate plea for help. The local authorities holding Charity's family could be bribed, but the $2,000 needed to release her sister and nephew was an insurmountable barrier. There was no way an impoverished farmer's daughter could raise the amount on her own.

It's in instances like these that I see God's heart for rescue most at work in the larger church body. Although $2,000 was an impossible number for Charity, it's an insignificant amount to many living here in the States. I went to work telling the story as soon as Debra passed the need along to me. Within a couple of days, supporters had provided enough for both family members to be released as well as additional medicine and food to help in the aftermath.

It was a wonderful reunion the day the two were set free. Although her sister would always be on a watch list, Charity had hopes that life could return to some form of normalcy. But the torture had done permanent damage. The residual effects of the wounds Charity's sister had sustained left her weak. Charity did all she could caring for her dying sister, worshiping beside her, and enjoying every moment of the precious time that had been redeemed for them. Despite her efforts, her sister died a year after she had been released.

Charity takes comfort knowing her sister is with the Lord, but is also well aware she may one day share in the same suffering. Her continued bravery has been well worth the risk and has produced incredible fruit in her community. In an impoverished country, her village is considered among the poorest but the thriving underground church she serves is growing.

Even orphaned street children have found refuge through Charity's care. Over the years, she has provided many nights of lodging and warm meals to kids who knock on her door. In a country where most doors remain closed to orphans in need, her home has become a beacon of light.

It's an amazing reminder to "never grow weary in doing good" (Gal. 6:9). It's also a reminder that a global body of believers is required to ensure these stories continue. Even now many others just like Charity are serving the villages under their care. They can do what they do because the church around the world chooses to support their mission.

Chapter 7 – The Cost of Owning a Bible

The cold of the prison cell quickly penetrated Joseph's thin clothes, chilling him to the bone. His body ached from the beating he had endured. His organs felt bruised and out of place and he was pretty sure his knee was broken beyond repair. Was this the end?

Joseph, a North Korean underground Christian, was arrested after being found with a digital media player. Digital devices such as tablets or smart phones are illegal to own for the average citizen due to their communication capabilities with the outside world. Possessing such a device without proper regulation can be a serious offence. Joseph's punishment of torture and a prison sentence came when officials found a Bible and other Christian resources loaded on his device.

Joseph had acquired the media player in China while traveling on a cross-border business permit. Unbeknown to the North Korean officials in charge of monitoring his business activities, Joseph had been visiting a covert safe house once he was safely across the China border. At the safe house, he had been given a meal, a quiet room to rest and stay warm, and, most importantly, discipleship in his secret faith in Christ.

Many Christian safe houses exist along the China/North Korea border. Chinese believers understand the threats of defying their own government in order to follow Jesus. Like a modern day version of Nazi controlled Europe, these brave men and women are making their homes available for North Korean escapees and those like Joseph with business permits.

Christians operating these safe houses risk their lives in this outreach. Those discovered harboring North Korean refugees are given prison sentences. Some have even been executed by

North Korean secret police. The secret police are sent into China to hunt down those who have escaped and those aiding in their rescue. Even with the threats they face, most safe house operators stay strong in their mission to help, knowing those they shelter have nowhere else to turn.

Joseph had visited the safe house on multiple occasions, each time studying the Bible intensively under the loving care of the Chinese hosts. He knew the risk he faced by taking the media player back inside North Korea when his travel permit expired, but he also knew that many in his underground church network desperately needed the hope it contained. The media player held an entire library of knowledge on its small hard drive, a vast spiritual treasure trove of digital text, audio, and video. The opportunity was too great to pass up.

On the floor of the prison cell, beaten and bloody, he'd questioned his actions. There was only one source of hope in that darkness preventing him from completely giving up. The gentle whisper of the Holy Spirit reminding him he was not alone.

Through God's incredible provision, on-site partners working with the safe house network learned of Joseph's imprisonment. A covert negotiation process began with the police overseeing the jail where Joseph had been detained. To his astonishment, Joseph was released not long after. Although badly shaken, he began recovering and wanted those who helped to know that his spirit remains firm in his faith.

Many digital Bibles, like the one Joseph carried, have infiltrated the closed North Korean borders without being confiscated. Even now, underground churches are secretly using these incredible tools to grow in their faith despite threats of severe persecution. They are priceless treasures of light in an environment desperate for spiritual food.

The next time you look over the multiple Bibles that line the shelves of your home, remember our North Korea brothers and sister in Christ and the price they would pay for that same privilege.

Tension filled the awkward reunion. Despite the customary pleasantries that began the meeting, Bo couldn't help remembering how Ju, his former business partner, had cheated him out of a lot of money. Bo also recalled how bitter and angry he felt by the betrayal. But now he was about to hand Ju another golden opportunity to betray him, and this time the stakes couldn't be higher.

Bo had been a successful Chinese businessman, trading goods across the border between China and North Korea. Ju had been his North Korean partner. Checking through his books one day Bo discovered Ju had been cheating him out of a lot of money. In outrage, Bo severed their business relationship.

A few years passed and, by God's grace, Bo and his wife Annie heard the gospel in China. They became ardent followers of Christ and even enrolled in a secret Chinese Bible school to anchor themselves more fully in their new faith. It was during those days of intense study that they first felt the Lord calling them to train North Korean believers to become undercover house church leaders. Bo knew his business connections in North Korea would give them access to people many others couldn't reach. The work would be very dangerous, even fatal if they were discovered. Bo and Annie counted this potential peril as the cost of following Jesus, and accepted the new mission.

The key to success, they felt, was enlisting the help of Ju, but this was no small task. They needed to persuade the estranged partner to become a believer and then join their discipleship training plans. It meant asking him to risk his life for the sake of the Gospel. Without him, there would be no one to communicate across the border on behalf of the underground church.

Bo and Annie hadn't spoken to Ju in years, and didn't know if he still harbored ill feelings toward Bo for the way he had severed the business partnership. They also had a much bigger problem: if Ju was unreceptive to the message of Jesus, he'd likely turn Bo and Annie over to authorities and reveal their larger plans.

Trusting that God would handle all the obstacles, Bo contacted Ju to arrange a meeting. Shocked that his former associate would reach out in peace to him after so many years, Ju accepted his invitation.

With hesitation conquered only by their faith, Bo and Annie carefully unfolded their personal story of redemption as Ju listened intently. They capped their testimony by extending an emotional olive branch of forgiveness to Ju. Blown away by the couple's unprecedented kindness, Ju repented of his own sin and committed his life to the One who had so deeply transformed his old friends.

Amazingly, Ju then began taking faith risks of his own by telling his family and extended relatives about Jesus. In just three years he led over 20 families to Christ who continued to meet in secret in his home.

Bo and Annie renewed their partnership with Ju, but this time to secretly transport North Korean believers and emergency relief supplies across the border. New Christians from Ju's underground church were smuggled into China for intensive three-week training and discipleship sessions under the Chinese couple. The spiritually hungry students would write key verses and truths they learned onto small pieces of paper, which they then hid in deep recesses of their clothing to smuggle back into North Korea.

Bo and Annie's border-crossing kingdom work has come at the price of arrests, interrogations and harsh beatings over the years. Even so, this heroic couple and the network of believers they disciple have stayed true to their calling and mission.

Chapter 9 – Smuggled Letters

It is with great joy that I am able to share the following letter from a North Korean Christian woman named Sun that was written for those who have supported her in secret over the years. Sun crossed the dangerous border area to visit a safe house in China, where she received both spiritual and physical food to bring back to her family in Christ inside North Korea.

Dear People of God,

I am Sun. I was born in a place where many North Koreans envy to live. But then my father was wrongly accused and we were exiled to a work camp overnight. We were in a living hell, going through countless struggles every day.

At that time, I did not know that God had a plan for my family. I had not known or believed in God. Then a miracle happened. My family's name was cleared of charges and we were released. Then my eldest sister was allowed to visit our aunt in China. While she was there she met a pastor and accepted Jesus Christ as her savior.

As soon as my sister returned, she asked me to believe in Jesus. At first, I was scared. But then, holding my sister's hands, I prayed to accept Jesus as my savior. My sister taught me the gospel and told me that my house was now a church.

When my neighbors are sick, I pray for them intensely. Amazingly, they get healed. Some of us gather together to worship in a dugout mud cellar made for Kimchi (spicy, fermented cabbage). Of course, we are risking our lives for our faith. When we do, we sing and read the Bible breathlessly, using our softest voices, lest someone hears us. The Holy Spirit has been working in us, and our church has been growing every day.

Truly, it was my greatest wish to come to China to study the

Bible deeply and worship the Lord freely in a loud voice. Even now, the members of our church back in North Korea are praying for me, taking turns every day. I would very much appreciate it if you can pray for me too.

Daughter of God,
Sun

Part 2: Breaking Out

Chapter 10 – Surviving Solo

Life is full of rough seasons, isn't it? Many of us have walked through the difficulty of this broken side of eternity where the road becomes long and the mountain steep. We are forced to crawl on our hands and knees just to make it another day. If we are honest, we've questioned God's presence during these seasons. It feels like we are surviving solo.

What if, even for just a moment, we were given the ability to see the invisible? What if we could view a divine orchestration over our lives when the world feels especially heavy? What if instead of abandonment, Jesus actually walks closer than ever with us as we navigate through rough seasons toward safety? What if a family of believers is right there ready to offer hope?

May Samuel's against-all-odds story of escape reveal the heart of our ever-present rescuing God...

It was past midnight and Samuel was standing on the riverbank looking back across the dark water now separating him from his home country North Korea. Adrenaline was pumping through his veins. He had made it! He had actually made it.

His friends told him that escape by crossing the border waters into China could not be done. Soldiers had been ordered to shoot anyone attempting to cross. An experienced guide could be hired to navigate around the many military foxholes lining the river's edge, but their fees were astronomical.

Samuel had beaten the odds by crossing an area of the border surrounded by mountains without the help of a guide. Although guard-posts were fewer in those regions, escapees choose to avoid mountainous crossing points as remote survival becomes necessary until shelter can be located. Most Chinese cities are more than three days journey on foot from the mountains and many perish from exhaustion and hunger.

But that's not all defectors face. Both Chinese and North Korean secret police arrest escapees when found and deport them back to an awaiting labor camp sentence. If that weren't enough, human traffickers also hunt and capture North Koreans in their vulnerability. Women are sold into the sex industry and men like Samuel are forced into slavery. They work in horrific conditions and face the threat of being turned over to the police if they fail to submit.

Samuel again defied logic by surviving not just three days, but an entire year along the dangerous China border region. The young man kept on the move, frequently changing locations and only gathering supplies when his presence could go unnoticed. But his solo journey had taken an emotional toll. More than anything, Samuel ached for a home and a family.

Many may see Samuel's survival as a fortunate defiance of the odds. However, what came next indicated that something much larger was at work. Through God's divine leading Samuel met another escapee and learned of a Christian operated safe house in the area.

After almost thirteen months on the run, Samuel finally felt a sense of peace as the home's hosts welcomed him with a warm meal and refuge. Within the walls of the safe house, he was introduced to Jesus and a family of Christians which extended around the world. It was more than he could ever have hoped for.

Samuel prayed and asked Christ to become his Savior. It was a priceless gift, but it would not be the last. The safe house hosts were able to offer Samuel safe passage to a country that would welcome him as a refugee. He is now living as a free man in South Korea.

Chapter 11 – The Walking Ghost

The four men walked in silence. They were always silent at this time of day, weary from hours of hard labor. John, a North Korean miner, trudged just behind his three coworkers watching the silhouettes created by their headlamps on the cavern walls. Lately he had been thinking about how much more real the shadows seemed than the walking ghosts he and his friends had become.

Slowly the shadows faded, consumed by growing sunlight which spilled though the mine's entrance. John placed his palm against his dirt-smeared face, protecting his eyes from the sun's brightness as the men emerged from the mine.

Though there were no shadows here, John could not shake the feeling that the small group still walked as ghosts in the daylight. It affirmed his resolution; he would not succumb to this reality. His three friends would be back tomorrow but John would not be among them.

He was going to escape North Korea.

That night John slept fitfully, tossing and turning with the nightmares that kept him from the comfort of rest, even after so many years. His dreams were terror filled memories of his first attempt as a boy to flee North Korea with his mother.

Desperate to leave behind the starvation that had taken many of his family and friends, 14 year old John and his mother had fled to China under the cover of night. But salvation continued to elude them in the new country. After months of living in hiding John and his mother were exhausted. Each day, his mother would leave to look for work, piecing together off-the-books jobs to earn enough money for their survival.

One day, John's mother never returned from a job where she had been working as a cleaner. John was frantic. After weeks of frenzied searching he still had not found a single trace of her. His hope was crushed completely when he was discovered by Chinese police and deported back to North Korea.

Thirteen years had passed since his capture, and still John wondered about the whereabouts of his mother. If the police had found her, she would have been deported like he had been to a North Korean labor camp. Surely, he would have been notified after his own arrest. Since this was not the case, her disappearance most likely meant one thing; human traffickers had abducted her.

John had heard the horror stories of North Korean women enslaved by traffickers. Some were forced to work in brothels. Some were sold as "wives" to desperate Chinese farmers. Others were locked in apartments and forced to do degrading things for Internet viewers. The thought of his mother trapped among those being abused pushed his determination all the more to return to China.

In the wee hours of the morning, John packed a few precious possessions and closed his front door, for what he hoped would be the last time. Under the cover of darkness, he retraced the steps he and his mother had taken over a decade earlier. Standing on the banks of the wide border river, he turned one last time to gaze upon the land that, like the mine, had almost swallowed him whole. Then taking a deep breath, he plunged into the cold waters.

God, with His great compassion, divinely intervened in John's story as he exited the river on the China side in those early morning hours. Kai, a leader in a modern day Underground

Railroad used to help North Koreans escape from China to freedom in South Korea, had decided to go for a walk along the river bank as sleep had been eluding him. The two ran into each other. After taking one look at John's soaked clothes, Kai immediately knew the stranger's story and offered to help.

Kai leads a small band of rough heroes, who offer hope to fleeing refugees like John through food, shelter, and most importantly the Gospel. Kai's methods of outreach are meticulous. He invests considerable amounts of time to develop relationship with North Korean escapees—both to flush out spies and to establish trusted friendships. Always intertwined in his communication is the message of Christ's deep love and sacrifice.

John spent a considerable amount of time with Kai and was deeply moved by the revelation of a God who loved him and had a plan for his life. As Kai discipled the North Korean in his new faith, the two discussed John's desire to find his mother. Although John had planned on searching for her while in China, Kai strongly cautioned against the undertaking, offering an alternative. If John used the Chinese Underground Railroad to safely relocate to South Korea, he could become a citizen and then return legally to continue his search.

Filled with hope, John felt the shadow of his past falling away. Like the darkness of the mine, he knew that his journey as a walking ghost was coming to an end, replaced by God's glorious light.

Chapter 12 – The Courier

As Aaron's cell phone rang with a tone he had set for a special foreign client, his heart began to beat fast. The Chinese man is a courier, a career field that requires him to be ready at any moment to provide transport. Last minute assignments were common in his line of work, but looking down at his phone, he knew the evening's contract would be far from normal.

Courier work in China had given Aaron a vast knowledge of routes across the country. He knew which options provided speed or sensitivity. As his knowledge grew, so had his opportunities within the business. In fact, friends had introduced him to a special form of courier service that would fully utilize his unique skill set.

On his first day driving for the "off the books" job, Aaron immediately had second thoughts. From the backseat, a scared pair of eyes looked at him in the rearview mirror. His cargo was a single man, a North Korean, who had escaped into China and was desperate to reach Southeast Asia. Aaron had learned that in a neutral country near the border, North Korean escapees could receive refugee status.

The man in the backseat had put his full trust in Aaron's expertise. If Chinese police had intercepted their car during the ten-day journey, Aaron would have been thrown in prison and his passenger sentenced to a labor camp in North Korea. It was long days of driving, but the two men had made it safely to the border without incident. Although neither spoke the other's language, Aaron saw immense gratitude in the North Korean's face.

That same gratitude from each of his passengers has kept Aaron in the special transportation business. For many years he has worked to ensure safe travel across China for escaping North Koreans.

Aaron let the client's ring tone chime once more and then pressed the answer button. He listened carefully as a man he knew only as "Mr. Lee" gave him details of a woman named Jenny and her child who were in great need.

Jenny and her son had recently arrived scared and exhausted at one of Mr. Lee's safe houses. After a brief time of counseling and care, Jenny disclosed her story to Mr. Lee and his wife. She had trusted a man on the border who promised her a prosperous life in China. The man turned out to be a human trafficker and once Jenny was smuggled across the border, she was sold to a Chinese farmer.

For over two years, Jenny lived as a slave to the man she was sold to. In captivity she gave birth to a son. Knowing the child stood little chance of ever having a normal life; she escaped and through sympathetic friends found Mr. Lee's safe house. But word reached the house that Jenny was on the Chinese police watch list. Her only option was to leave the border city as soon as possible.

"I'll take the job," Aaron spoke into the phone receiver. The sigh of relief from Mr. Lee confirmed he'd made the right decision.

The city was silent in the early morning hours as Aaron pulled his car in back of the apartment complex where the safe house was located. After a few moments, three figures emerged from a darkened stairwell entrance, one clutching a small child close to her chest. A couple in their mid-forties, Aaron assumed to be Mr. Lee and his wife, opened the backdoor of his car, illuminating Jenny and her son as they were quickly ushered inside. The couple gave her one last hug, closed the car door, and then slipped back into the stairwell as quietly as they had come.

Aaron looked in his rearview mirror at the familiar sight. Staring back at him were the scared eyes of the two refugees. He smiled and gave a reassuring nod. Putting the car in drive, he pulled out onto the open road. Another journey had begun, lives were again in his hands, and he was determined to ensure their safe arrival.

Chapter 13 – The Refugee's Secret

One of my favorite parts of this ministry over the last decade is meeting North Koreans we have helped bring to freedom. From the moment refugees like Jenny and her son enter the care of a safe house, they are prayed over by our support network. Additional calls for prayer are sent out as they enter the care of couriers like Aaron and begin the dangerous journey across China.

Not all of those we have helped make it to the border region where they can be turned over to friendly ambassadors. But those who do, most often choose to relocate to South Korea, where they are given citizenship and government assistance while they rebuild. The prosperity of South Korea stands in stark contrast to how many escapees lived in their former country. Post- traumatic stress disorder is very common among North Korean escapees as they struggle to integrate into their new lives.

The South Korean church plays a vital role in the rehabilitation process. They are a shining light of community and support in a new world that can feel very foreign, cold and unwelcoming to North Koreans. It's here where I am able to play an active role in the ministry process as a representative of the western church.

I've traveled many times to South Korea to meet with escapees we have helped. Their stories are all powerful, but maybe none so much as Hana's.

Far off the busy South Korean streets, I sat quietly opposite Hana, a North Korean escapee who agreed to meet with me to tell her story. Hana absent-mindedly fidgeted with the scarf around her neck as she waited awkwardly, visibly uncomfortable. The scarf was much too warm for the late spring rendezvous, but very effective for covering her secret. It was a secret I was about to learn.

Growing up inside North Korea, food was scarce for Hana's family. When her husband died from sickness due to malnutrition, she began to question what might exist outside of the closed North Korean borders. Eventually mustering the courage to bribe a hungry border guard, Hana slipped quietly into China to look for a better life.

Just one week later Chinese police captured her. Bound in chains, Hana was forced back inside North Korea and labeled a traitor. As she waited for her punishment, authorities discovered that Hana's grandmother had been identified as a Christian. Although Hana emphatically professed the truth that she had no knowledge of the religion, guards began mercilessly torturing her, demanding that she confess her belief in the forbidden faith.

With deep anguish in her eyes, Hana recounts being strapped to a chair and then raised up off the floor by a chain pulley, only to be dropped violently, bruising her bones and muscles with the intense trauma. Wire was strung around her neck and then violently yanked tight, choking the air from her windpipe.

Hana momentarily paused her retelling to again fidget with the scarf around her neck. It was then that I realized its purpose: to hide the area where the wire had cut into her delicate skin. The scars will forever remind her of those hellish days.

The battered woman's anger could have been directed toward her grandmother for the undeserved pain, but Hana's memory of the old woman's gentle singing quickly became her only comfort in prison. Throughout her torture, Hana would hum those same melodies, using them to retain her sanity. Later, she would realize that those melodies were old Korean gospel hymns, carrying words that would one day bring her true freedom.

Hana was eventually set free. Completely disillusioned with the lies her country had told her, she could think of nothing else but escape.

The details of her harrowing journey to leave North Korea behind once and for all make a powerful story in and of themselves, but after almost a year on the run, Hana finally made it to South Korea. Once there she was introduced to a church community that embraces North Korean refugees. Although hostile to the gospel at first, Hana found her heart softening with each act of love the church offered her. It wasn't long before she embraced the faith of her grandmother and asked Jesus to be her Savior.

When visiting with North Koreans who have escaped, I often ask what they hope to do in the future now that they're free. Hana's answer surprised me. She said she hopes to one day lead a team of missionaries back into North Korea to help build a church community for those remaining in darkness!

Light in the darkness ... hope for the very persecutors who left her with scars. It's the kind of story only Jesus could write.

Hana's sacrifice to return to set free the very people who tried to break her is enough to humble anyone. It's during these meetings when I ask myself if there really is anything I have to offer this brave future missionary.

There is. You see, North Korean escapees arrive in South Korea completely brainwashed to the outside world. They've been told Westerners are the enemy, capable of horrific brutality. Each time I sit with a North Korean I have the opportunity to speak against that lie. So do you. They need our compassionate touch. They need our sincere prayers. Each of these interactions sends a powerful message that a larger church across the world cares deeply for them. They are not alone. They are part of a family in Christ.

Because of my time with Hana, she now has the ability to carry that message back to our hurting brothers and sisters still trapped inside North Korea.

Part 3: In-between

Chapter 14 – North Korea Coming to Us

Throughout this book, you've read stories of those who are able to offer hope by breaking into the closed borders of North Korea. You've also read about those who risk their lives to aid escapees who break out. But there is a third category of active ministry that is desperately needed by North Koreans who find themselves caught in-between captivity and freedom.

What if North Koreans were brought out of the darkness into countries where more freedom existed and where the salvation message could be delivered with less fear of persecution? Incredibly enough, this very thing is happening and a small team of Eastern European Christians is taking advantage of every opportunity.

As North Korea's dying economy continues to erode, the government has sought new ways of generating financial resources. One of these methods involves loaning its work force to allied nations. The work assigned is primarily hard-labor projects that reduce men to little more then slaves. Any wages a worker earns doing manual labor are taxed by the greedy North Korean government at the ridiculous rate of 80% or more. A worker may earn as little as 300 dollars for an entire year of work. Still, the laborers sign up for the program, many knowing it will be the only way to provide for their families back home.

By the time a North Korean worker reaches their assigned city or remote hard-labor worksite, most will have used up their meager rations. They are penniless, hungry and scared in a foreign country.

In 2004 a small Eastern European church, began to see North Korean workers arriving in their city. A compassionate man named Erik pastors a church and had a heart to share the Gospel with the North Korean people. He had struggled with how to best accomplish his vision, as it was impossible for him and his church to lead an open mission trip inside the closed county. Suddenly the very people he wished to minister to had arrived on his doorstep.

What the church observed broke their heart. Workers often endured bitterly cold weather conditions without proper clothing. Their diets consisted of little more then a basic starch, cheap vegetables, and some flavorings for taste. Most of the men appeared far too under- nourished for the hard labor they participated in on a daily basis.

Before Erik could begin his newfound ministry, he had to address a big challenge. When North Korean workers are sent outside of their country, they are assigned a monitoring agent working for the government called a "minder." The key to reaching the workers was through relationship with these minders, most of whom were given strict orders not to allow the workers any outside influence.

Erik's team began to look for any signs of compassion from the minders in charge of the men. Approaching with caution, the ministry team asked a very simple question: could the team provide free resources for the physical needs of the workers? To the churches' surprise, many minders began allowing limited access to the men under their charge, but always under a watchful eye.

During the first outreach trips, the ministry team from the church focused on a nearby train station where workers waited, sometimes for days, for continued transport to their work-sites.

The laborers were held in an isolated room in the station to avoid direct interaction with national citizens. The room was small and the workers huddled together surrounded with the few possessions they had been allowed to bring. They sat quietly, limiting their words for fear of punishment by the minders. Eyes on the floor, shoulders drooped, they waited for the next leg of their journey.

The fear the team sensed from the workers as they entered that room was an immediate hurdle. How were they going to show the love they wished to bring when such a great wall had been put in place? Erik knew they had to at least try. The small team passed out meals they had prepared including rice, seasoned meats, and vegetables. Although the workers were experiencing hunger pangs, many refused to accept the gift, scared of the repercussions their interaction with a foreigner might incur.

Erik wasn't pushy with the gifts. Realizing a more gentle approach was needed, the team placed the food in the middle of the room and after quickly passing a message of love through a translator, they left as quickly as they had come.

Years later, the minders have grown to trust Erik and his ministry team, allowing them to spend time alone with the workers. Without the constraints of the guard's constant presence, the team is able to freely share the Gospel message behind their gifts of love. They have even developed a secret booklet to pass out, which clearly outlines Christ's sacrifice for our salvation.

A single North Korean worker may pass though Erik's city as many as four times on their journey to and from North Korea. The ministry team uses these opportunities to develop relationships with the men, each time further developing the story of the Gospel. The workers ask questions and genuinely listen as the team answers. Some of them ask for prayer. On occasion, the church has even led times of worship, singing and teaching hymns to the workers in their native language.

When you step back to observe the larger picture, you begin to see just how unique this ministry opportunity is. Each worker who receives the Gospel seed planted by Erik and his team becomes a Trojan horse for the light of Christ as they return back to their country. Erik's team may never enter the closed borders of North Korea, but the fruit of their labor will.

The light of the Gospel cannot be stopped, and one way or another it will reach those who need to hear it.

Chapter 15 – Monsters in a Foreign Land

Dae lay curled in a ball on the dirty ground, struggling to maintain consciousness. He could taste warm blood running down the many open cuts that now marked his face. He struggled to breathe as his aching body made him painfully aware of his broken ribs. Although he felt the fear of being beaten by a pair of unknown attackers, he was not surprised.

The young North Korean man had been told stories of the world that existed beyond the closed borders of his home country. He had heard that life outside North Korea would be a harsh, brutal existence. With a starving family to take care of and no work available in his hometown, Dae had laid his fears aside to participate in the government labor program with an allied nation.

It took days for his train to finally arrive at the first city in the nation where he had been assigned. Feeling his anxiety growing, Dae stayed close to the other workers as the group waited for their next train. Every so often, he would catch a glimpse of a local man or woman through the station windows. Although their lives appeared more normal then he had been led to believe, he still remained cautious.

For hours, the men waited. Dae did his best to ignore his empty stomach but the growing need to empty his bladder began to be unbearable. Unable to ignore the discomfort any longer, Dae received the approval of his government-assigned guard and made his way to a public restroom located just outside the train station. He was surprised to see a woman sitting at the entrance. He watched as patrons paid a few coins to the woman and then were allowed admittance. His heart immediately sank. Along with his food ration, he had also used all of his minimal travel money. He couldn't afford to use the bathroom.

Looking around, Dae hurriedly made his way to the back of the restrooms, concealing himself as best as he could in the bushes that lined the building. He quickly relieved himself, hoping no one had seen his desperate act. As he turned back toward the train station, he was suddenly face-to-face with two local men. Although he could not understand the angry words that spilled from their mouths, he could see by their clenched fists and hate-filled stares that he had committed a great offense. He closed his eyes, praying to an unknown God for some mercy in the monsters before him and that somehow he would see his family again.

Dae was a North Korean worker who was beaten to near death in the same city where Erik and his church led their outreach. The team was devastated when they learned the news. The incident gave them new resolve to share the love of Jesus Christ so that the Gospel message is the first thing experienced beyond the walls of North Korea. As a result of Dae's horrific experience, the team has added toilet tickets to their gifts for the workers, which can be used at the public restroom.

New doors continue to open as stories spread throughout the church network connected to Erik's group. New teams are taking up the same mission to reach needy laborers assigned to some of the most remote regions of the country. Although the devil would love to keep the North Korean men living in fear and slavery, light is invading the darkness.

Chapter 16 – Ruth's Redemption

Is there anything more comforting than the warm embrace of a father? Without words, a father's arms can convey safety, strength, and a sense that no matter what troubles or dangers lurk in the darkness, everything will be okay.

Yet there are those of us who have been robbed of this comfort. Many of our stories include abandonment by disconnected fathers. Worse, some of us carry deep scars from physical abuse where only warm inviting hands should have existed.

And yet even in these broken stories, God is showing up to bring redemption. He is still at work, even an ocean away on the North Korean border.

The North Korean sex-trafficking trade has been growing larger each year as many women are tricked into illegally crossing the border as slaves. Their stories are typical of those around the globe who have been trafficked. Most are promised a better life, well paid jobs, and more money than they have ever had in their entire lives. Instead, North Korean women are sold to merchants, pimps, and isolated farmers looking for wives. These women have no choice but to obey their captors or risk being sent back to North Korea as traitors.

But the women aren't the only victims in this dark industry.

Hundreds of children are born every year as a result of this slavery. The boys and girls are abused, abandoned, and face a bleak future on the lonely streets. China is especially prone to this underground problem. In recent years the number of orphaned North Korean children has grown into the thousands. Gangs of these children roam the streets stealing and looting to survive.

The problem became so prevalent, that China secretly reached out to non-profit religious groups for help. China has policies against granting citizenship to children born from undocumented people living in their country (including North Korean sex slaves). Miraculously, Chinese officials have chosen to bend these rules when it comes to North Korean orphans. This is a rare privilege that offers education, medical attention, and other human rights. As a result, small orphanages have been developed along the border by loving Christian foster parents who care for as many North Korean orphans as their homes will hold.

When I visited one of these orphanages, I was surprised at what I found. The house sits on a wooded hillside, overlooking a picturesque valley. It is a place of warmth and life, with a beautiful interior and space for community and play. The laughter of children fills the halls. For a moment I was taken aback. This home stood in stark contrast the many cold images conjured up by the word "orphanage."

Instead of distant and withdrawn children who have endured the horrors of an abusive childhood, I was greeted with smiles and playful games.

The especially vibrant Ruth quickly stole my heart. As I listened to her story, it was hard to imagine that just a month earlier, the four year old had been abandoned. Her mother, a North Korean woman, had been sold as a wife to Ruth's father, who worked as a local Chinese farmer. During a crackdown, Chinese authorities had raided the farm and arrested Ruth's mother. She was taken to the border and handed over to North Korean police. Knowing that his purchased bride would never return, Ruth's father had abandoned the young girl on the streets.

How could anyone give up such a precious life? How could a father turn his back on a little one who desperately needed his provision? Though our earthly fathers may fail us, there is a redeemer who has gone to great lengths to purchase our lives and bring us into His loving care.

A redeemer is one who claims something or someone by paying the debt or ransom set against it. This picture is beautifully painted in an Old Testament story about a young woman who also shared the name Ruth. After losing her husband she found herself an alien in a foreign land. Her only hope for the future came from a man named Boaz who saw her plight and offered to pay the necessary price so she might come under his love and care.

I realized that day in the orphanage that little Ruth had faced a similar fate. She was in a foreign land without family or any hope of survival. Just as Boaz redeemed the biblical character, the Heavenly Father had redeemed little Ruth so that she might have a hope and a future.

Chapter 17 – Safe In Her Father's Arms

Adelynn is another little North Korean girl living in the border orphanage I visited. Her shy eyes, complemented by a partially hidden smile, gazed curiously up into my own. She had been the first to see me as I entered the warm house. She watched my movements, hiding behind her foster mother's kitchen apron. A smile spread across my face to match hers, and I waved to show I was a friend.

Adelynn's beauty is a constant reminder of God's ability to bring light into even the darkest places on earth. As we sat in the comfort of her new home listening to her story, I quickly realized that things could have turned out drastically different for the two-year-old North Korean.

Adelynn was born just a short distance from the orphanage, across the river in North Korea. Although only a few miles separated her from the land of her birth, the two worlds could not have been more different. Like most North Korean parents, Adelynn's mother and father lived with the very real possibility that they would one day die of starvation.

Adelynn's parents illegally crossed the river separating North Korea from China in an effort to find a new life. But existence inside China was filled with a new kind of danger, as they tried to avoid the watchful eye of Chinese border guards and secret North Korean police. Living in hiding, Adelynn's parents were able to gain a few allies among sympathetic Chinese locals who helped them find food and shelter.

Just before my visit to the orphanage, the unthinkable had happened. Adelynn's mother and father had disappeared without a trace.

Chinese neighbors might not have given the sudden disappearance of the family a second thought. But they had left something of importance behind ... scared little Adelynn, alone in a foreign land, crying for her mommy and daddy. Full of compassion, the neighbors knew they could not simply leave her there alone. They brought her to the doorstep of the orphanage hopeful that the Christians living there would take her in.

The little girl was, of course, welcomed into the family. Looking over at Adelynn, I knew she was finally safe. As if to confirm my thoughts, her adorable giggle filled the room as she watched us in amusement, safe in the embrace of her foster father's arms.

Part 4: Now What?

Chapter 18 — Your Part in the Story Matters

Until the devil's dying breath, he will fight to destroy the bride of Christ. If you are a follower of Jesus, that includes you. Why? He knows that as a carrier of the Holy Spirit, you have the ability to bring light to the most hostile areas around the world, including North Korea. You can be a hero for the Kingdom of God.

What is our initial response to this revelation? "Me, a hero? No way!"

Many of us struggle to accept the fact that we play a vital role in God's Kingdom. One of the greatest deceptions of the enemy is to make us believe the war does not exist. As a result, we walk through life unaware of his attacks on us and unaware of our true power in Christ.

I once was right there, but working alongside those rescuing the persecuted over these many years has changed my perspective drastically. You see, although our partners may be physically inside hostile areas, they know they are ultimately fighting a spiritual war. They know the larger body of Christ is their lifeline. Without your support and prayers, they have no chance of succeeding.

I want to invite you to embrace the role you've been offered and see yourself as a hero. For those of you who have only watched from the sidelines, now is your time to join the fight. For those who have found yourselves off the battlefield, it's time to reengage, to realize how much you are needed.

Part of the proceeds from this book go directly to those you've read about who serve on the frontlines. By purchasing a copy, you have already joined the effort to bring the light of Christ into North Korea. And there are many more ways to get involved through some great faith-based organizations. Who knows, you may even end up with a surprise story like mine of deeper involvement than you ever thought possible.

Hope to see you out there!

About the Author

For over a decade Scott Croft has worked for multiple faith-based non-profits who serve persecuted Christians. He lives with his beautiful bride in their U.S. based home where they speak, write, and produce media to help equip the global body of Christ to join the modern rescue story of the Gospel. Scott has frequently traveled to help coordinate undercover efforts in some of the most hostile areas around the globe including North Korea. The book you are holding is a collection of the short stories he has written documenting the brave men and women who risk their lives to bring light to the most persecuted nation on earth.

Made in the USA
Coppell, TX
03 June 2021